FREEDOM'S PROMISE

ONEY
JUDGE

ESCAPE FROM SLAVERY AND THE PRESIDENT'S HOUSE

BY DUCHESS HARRIS, JD, PHD
WITH LINDSAY WYSKOWSKI

Core Library

An Imprint of Abdo Publishing
abdobooks.com

Cover image: Ona "Oney" Judge escaped slavery in the late 1700s.

abdocorelibrary.com

Published by Abdo Publishing, a division of ABDO, PO Box 398166, Minneapolis, Minnesota 55439. Copyright © 2019 by Abdo Consulting Group, Inc. International copyrights reserved in all countries. No part of this book may be reproduced in any form without written permission from the publisher. Core Library™ is a trademark and logo of Abdo Publishing.

Printed in the United States of America, North Mankato, Minnesota
092018
012019

Cover Photo: Laura Freeman
Interior Photos: Laura Freeman, 1, 18; Beth J. Harpaz/AP Images, 5, 43; Daniel M. Silva/ Shutterstock Images, 6–7; akg-images/Newscom, 8; North Wind Picture Archives, 12–13, 15; Red Line Editorial, 17, 29; Photo Josse/Leemage/Corbis Historical/Getty Images, 20–21; John M. Chase/Shutterstock Images, 23; GraphicaArtis/Archive Photos/Getty Images, 26–27; Independent Picture Service/Universal Images Group Editorial/Getty Images, 31; Kelsey Neukum/Shutterstock Images, 34–35; Hulton Archive/Getty Images, 38

Editor: Maddie Spalding
Series Designer: Claire Vanden Branden

Library of Congress Control Number: 2018949779

Publisher's Cataloging-in-Publication Data

Names: Harris, Duchess, author. | Wyskowski, Lindsay, author.
Title: Oney Judge: escape from slavery and the president's house / by Duchess Harris and Lindsay Wyskowski.
Other title: Escape from slavery and the president's house
Description: Minneapolis, Minnesota : Abdo Publishing, 2019 | Series: Freedom's promise | Includes online resources and index.
Identifiers: ISBN 9781532117732 (lib. bdg.) | ISBN 9781641856072 (pbk) | ISBN 9781532170591 (ebook)
Subjects: LCSH: Judge, Oney--Juvenile literature. | Fugitive slaves--United States-- Biography--Juvenile literature. | Fugitive slaves--Legal status, laws, etc.--United States-- Biography--Juvenile literature.
Classification: DDC 306.362092 [B]--dc23

CONTENTS

A LETTER FROM DUCHESS

The first president of the United States, George Washington, and his wife, Martha, owned Ona "Oney" Judge. The Washingtons lived in Philadelphia, Pennsylvania. Many students forget that Philadelphia was the nation's first capital.

One of the goals of this book is to explain the role that free black people played in Philadelphia. Enslaved black people such as Judge escaped slavery and were sometimes assisted by other black people.

Judge did not want to be enslaved by Martha Washington or her granddaughter, Eliza. Judge was a brave woman. Not only did she free herself, she escaped the president of the United States.

I did not learn about Judge myself until 2015. So my hope is that this book introduces you to a lesser-known American hero who deserves to be remembered and read about. Join me on a journey that tells the story of the promise of freedom.

Duchess Harris

A display in Philadelphia, Pennsylvania, tells Oney Judge's story.

CHAPTER
ONE

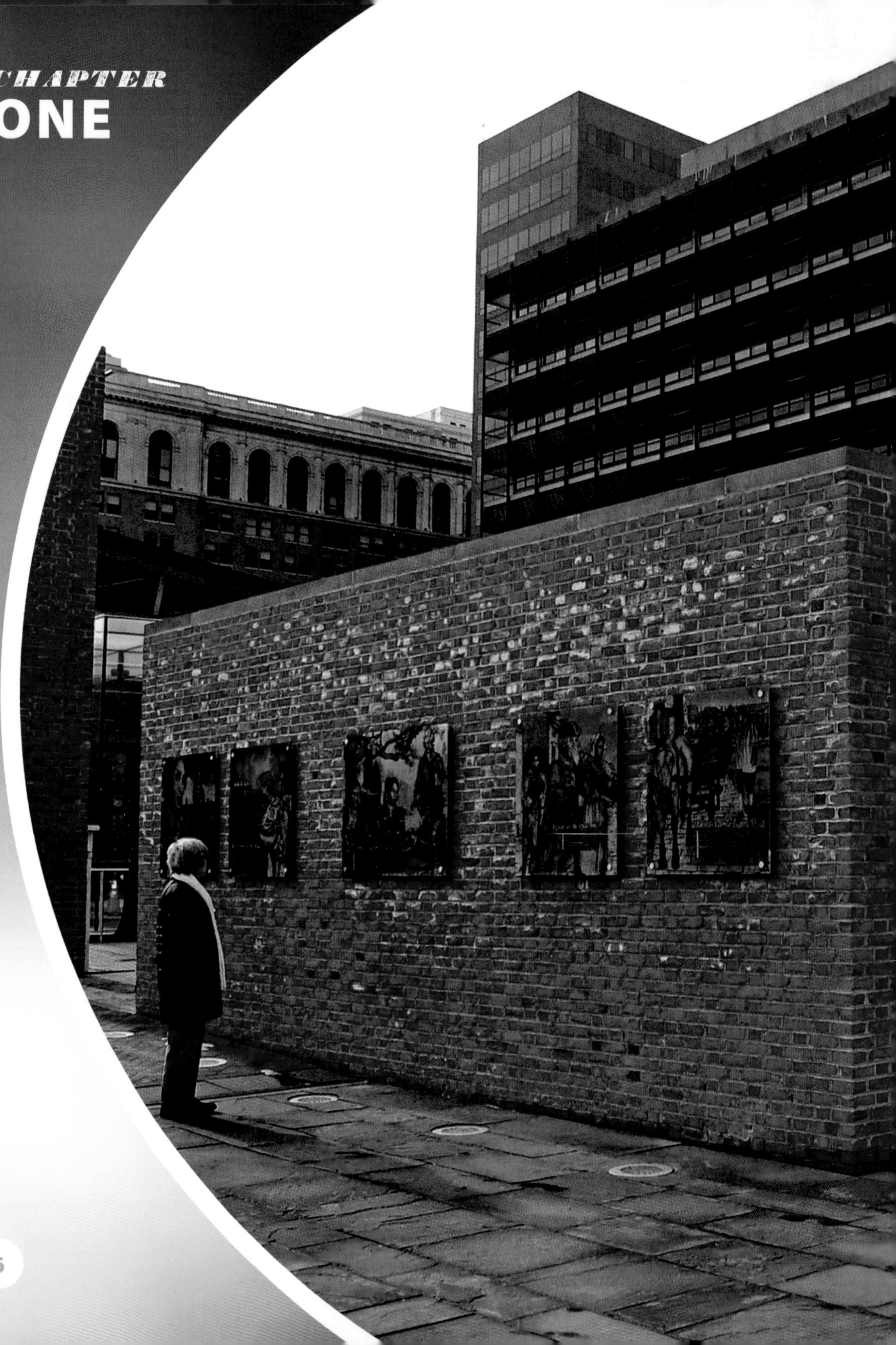

ESCAPING SLAVERY

President George Washington and his wife, Martha, sat down for dinner in the presidential mansion. The date was May 21, 1796. It seemed like an ordinary day.

The presidential mansion was in Philadelphia, Pennsylvania. Washington and his family lived there part-time. At the time, Philadelphia was the capital of the United States. Washington was the nation's first president. Soon he and his family would travel to Mount Vernon in Alexandria, Virginia, for the summer. The Washingtons had another home there.

Today an exhibit stands on the site of the former presidential mansion in Philadelphia, Pennsylvania, where the Washingtons lived.

Martha married George Washington in 1759.

Like many other wealthy people in the late 1700s, the Washingtons were slaveholders. Enslaved people worked for the Washington family inside their home and on their farm. These people were considered the Washingtons' property. They did everything the Washingtons told them to do. They would soon be traveling to Mount Vernon with the family.

Ona "Oney" Judge was enslaved by the Washingtons. While the Washingtons prepared to go to Mount Vernon, Judge had other plans. She was

22 years old. She had been enslaved her entire life. She decided she wanted a new life. Today was the day she was going to run away.

BREAKING FREE

Judge had recently overheard that the Washingtons planned to give her to a new slaveholder. The new slaveholder was Martha's granddaughter, Eliza Law. Eliza had just gotten married. Judge was to be given to Eliza and her husband as a wedding gift.

TRANSPORTATION IN THE 1790s

In the late 1700s, people did not have many options when they wanted to travel. The first railroad in the United States was not built until 1830. Enslaved people who wanted to escape had limited transportation options. They could run away on horse or on foot. Sometimes enslaved people escaped by ship. Until steamboats were invented in the early 1800s, ships relied on sails to propel them through water. Sailing ships could be slow, especially when winds were not strong.

Judge did not want to be passed off to another slaveholder. Eliza and her husband could sell Judge or treat her poorly. But Judge did not have a choice. She had to follow orders. Judge knew she had to do something. She wanted to be free and make her own choices.

In Philadelphia, Judge had met people who showed her a new way of life. The city was home to the largest free black community in the North. More than 2,000 free African Americans lived there. Judge saw how they lived. They opened schools and became teachers. They worked as doctors, bakers, and musicians. These people would help Judge escape.

While the Washingtons ate their dinner, Judge approached the front door. It was risky to leave without permission. If Judge was caught, she would be in trouble. She could be whipped or sold. But the Washingtons were distracted by the evening meal. They did not see her leave.

Judge slipped out of the house quietly. She had packed clothing in advance. Her things were waiting with a friend, a member of the free African American community. Then Judge boarded a ship on the Delaware River. The ship was bound for New Hampshire. But Judge did not know her destination until it was time to leave. Free African Americans had arranged her passage.

By the time anyone realized she was missing, Judge was far away. She had escaped from the president of the United States. She was on her way to the life she desired.

SLAVERY IN EARLY AMERICA

The United States became an independent country in 1776. Before it was a country, it was made up of colonies. People from Great Britain and other parts of Europe settled there.

In the 1600s, British settlers brought enslaved people to North America. The British had captured these people in Africa. The settlers enslaved men, women, and children. Enslaved people arrived on ships along the Atlantic Coast. The ships docked in places such as Jamestown, a settlement in the Virginia colony. Dutch settlers also brought

Enslaved people were sold to slaveholders at auctions.

SLAVERY AROUND THE WORLD

Slavery was not limited to the North American colonies. In the 1400s, Portuguese slave traders traveled to Africa and captured people. The slave traders sold enslaved people in many European countries. These countries included England, Spain, France, Denmark, Sweden, and the Netherlands. Eventually, nearly 400,000 Africans were transported to North American colonies. Slave traders took many more enslaved people across the Atlantic Ocean to South America and the Caribbean. In total, millions of Africans were loaded onto ships and sent to other countries. Some countries finally began to end slavery in the early 1800s.

enslaved people to New Netherland, the Dutch colony in North America.

Enslaved people worked for settlers on their farms and inside their homes. The settlers considered their slaves to be their property. Slaveholders did not pay enslaved people for their work. Enslaved people did not have many rights. They worked six days a week, from the time the sun rose until it set.

Enslaved people worked long hours and did hard labor.

Enslaved people often worked outside in the heat. They tended crops of tobacco, cotton, sugarcane, and other plants. They also cooked, cleaned, and did other household chores. Many enslaved people hoped to be free one day. But laws were put in place to prevent that from happening.

SLAVE LAWS

Throughout the 1600s and 1700s, the colonies created rules that limited what Africans and other people of color could do. In 1639 one rule said that people of African descent could not own guns or ammunition. Another rule made it illegal for Africans to own livestock. It was illegal to teach an enslaved person to read or write. These rules made life harder for enslaved people.

SLAVERY IN AMERICA

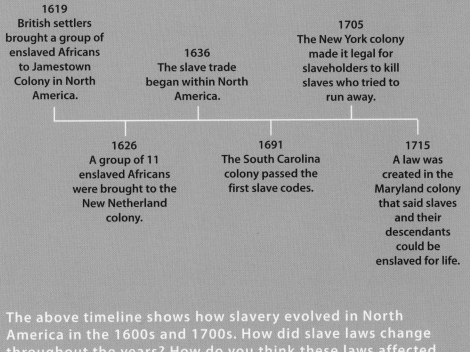

1619
British settlers brought a group of enslaved Africans to Jamestown Colony in North America.

1636
The slave trade began within North America.

1705
The New York colony made it legal for slaveholders to kill slaves who tried to run away.

1626
A group of 11 enslaved Africans were brought to the New Netherland colony.

1691
The South Carolina colony passed the first slave codes.

1715
A law was created in the Maryland colony that said slaves and their descendants could be enslaved for life.

The above timeline shows how slavery evolved in North America in the 1600s and 1700s. How did slave laws change throughout the years? How do you think these laws affected Oney Judge?

In 1662 the Virginia colony made a law that declared slavery hereditary. This meant that the children of enslaved people were considered slaves themselves at birth. The law also made it legal for slavery to last a person's entire life.

More slave laws were made in Virginia in 1705. These were called slave codes. The slave codes defined

Born into a longstanding system of slavery, Judge sought to gain her freedom.

who could be considered a slave. Anyone who had

African or Native American ancestry could be enslaved.

Another law said that if a slaveholder killed an enslaved

person who had tried to escape, the slaveholder

would not be punished. Enslaved people were not

allowed to leave the slaveholders' property unless they

had written permission. Other laws imposed harsh punishments for enslaved people. Enslaved people who had been found guilty of robbery could be whipped, and their ears could be cut off. These slave codes were adopted in other colonies too.

These laws meant fewer people could become free. As enslaved people had children, the number of enslaved people grew. By 1790 approximately 698,000 people were enslaved in the United States. Judge was one of them.

FURTHER EVIDENCE

Chapter Two covers the history of slavery in early America. What was one of the main points of this chapter? What evidence is included to support this point? Read the article at the website below. Does the information on the website support the main point of the chapter? Does it present new evidence?

SLAVERY IN AMERICA
abdocorelibrary.com/oney-judge

CHAPTER
THREE

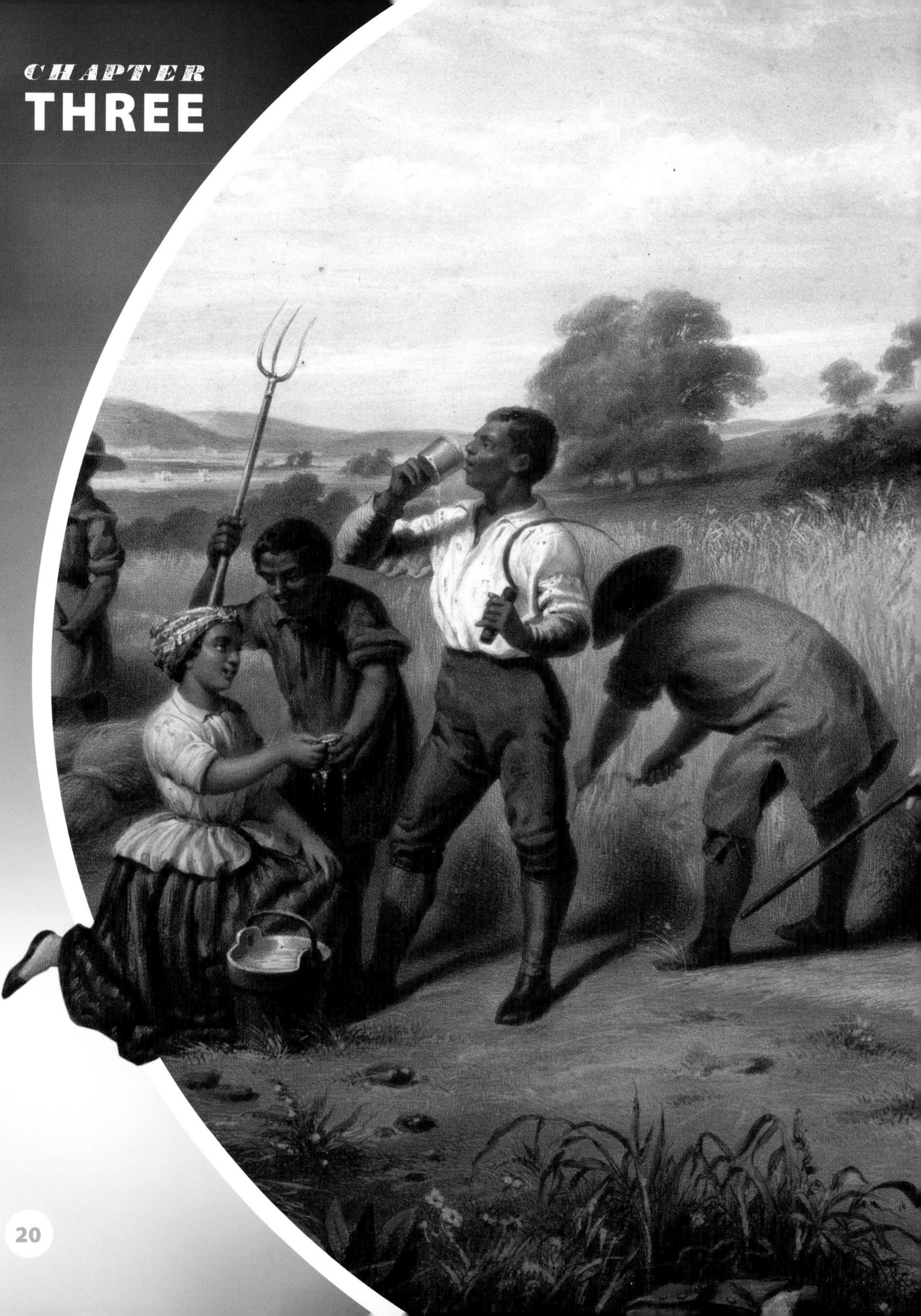

ONEY'S EARLY YEARS

Geoge Washington became a slaveholder at age 11. His father gave him ten enslaved people. Over the years, he brought more enslaved people to Mount Vernon, where he lived.

George married Martha Custis in 1759. Martha had been married once before. Her first husband died, leaving all his property to her. This inheritance included more than 80 enslaved people. Eventually the Washingtons enslaved more than 300 people at Mount Vernon. One of these enslaved people was an African American woman

Enslaved people tended to George Washington's land at Mount Vernon. While some historical artwork shows slaves smiling at their duties, the reality of life under slavery was harsh and brutal.

George Washington was not the only US president who was also a slaveholder. Twelve of the first eighteen presidents were slaveholders at some point in their lives. Some of them publicly said that enslaving people was wrong. Washington said this too. But that did not stop them from being slaveholders themselves.

named Betty. Betty was a seamstress. She sewed clothes for the Washingtons.

ONEY'S FAMILY

Oney Judge was born around 1773. Betty was her mother. Children born to enslaved women became the property of their mothers' slaveholders. Betty was the Washingtons' property, so Oney became the Washingtons' property as well.

Oney's father was a white Englishman named Andrew. He had worked as an indentured servant for the Washingtons. He had agreed to work for four years at Mount Vernon in exchange for money to cover his travel from England to the colonies as well as his shelter

Enslaved people at Mount Vernon lived in small cabins, some of which have been reconstructed on the site today.

and food. At the end of his four years at Mount Vernon, Andrew left to start his own farm. Oney and her mother had to remain at Mount Vernon.

ONEY'S CHILDHOOD

As a young girl, Oney lived in a part of Mount Vernon called the Quarters. It was also known as the House for Families. Other enslaved people also lived there, including Oney's half siblings. Oney had two half brothers and two half sisters. Betty worked all day. Oney and her siblings likely did not see their mother much.

Like her mother, Oney had a talent for sewing. The Washingtons moved Oney into their main house when she was ten years old. She worked as a seamstress for a few years. Then she became Martha's personal maid. She took care of Martha every day. Oney helped Martha get dressed, take baths, and brush her hair.

TRAVEL

When George became president in 1789, he moved to New York with Martha. Two of Martha's grandchildren from her first marriage moved with them. Martha would not go to New York without Oney. Oney was one of seven enslaved people who traveled with the Washingtons to New York. The rest of the enslaved people stayed behind to take care of Mount Vernon.

Oney traveled with Martha wherever she went. When Martha went to stores or to visit friends, Oney had to go too. Trips with the Washingtons helped open Oney's eyes to a whole new world.

EXPLORE ONLINE

Chapter Three explores Oney's childhood at George Washington's home at Mount Vernon. The website below gives more information about the lives of enslaved people at Mount Vernon. How is the information from the website the same as the information in Chapter Three? What new information did you learn from the website?

GEORGE WASHINGTON'S MOUNT VERNON: SLAVERY
abdocorelibrary.com/oney-judge

CHAPTER FOUR

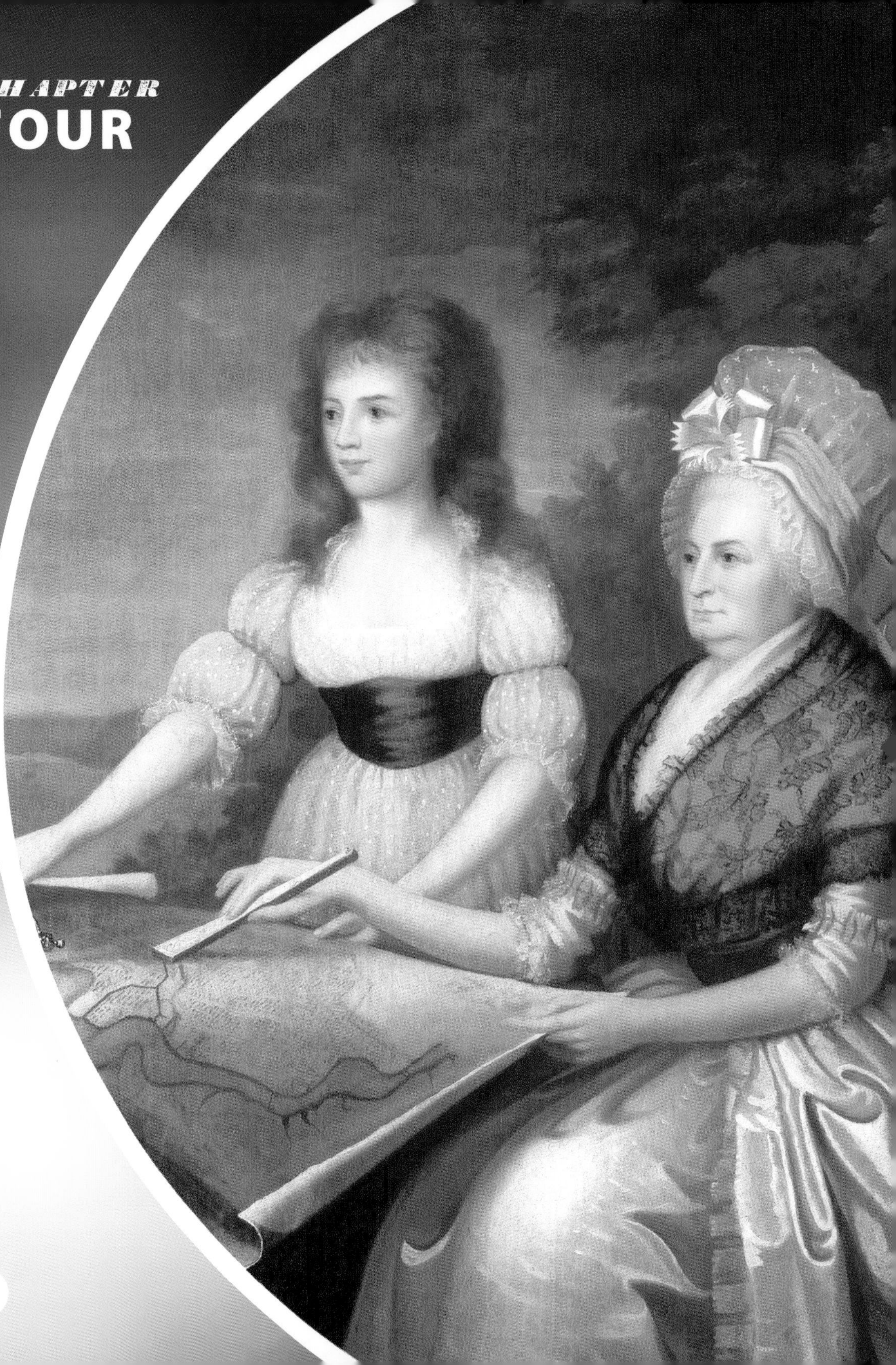

ESCAPE PLAN

Oney Judge lived with the Washingtons in New York for one year. Then the Washingtons moved to Philadelphia. But Judge and others enslaved by the Washingtons had to make regular trips back to Mount Vernon. This was because of a law that was passed in Pennsylvania in 1780. The law was called An Act for the Gradual Abolition of Slavery. It said that enslaved people who lived in Philadelphia for more than six months would be considered residents. They would become free. This law was meant to eventually end slavery. Pennsylvania was the first colony to pass this type of law.

The Washingtons lived with Martha's grandchildren and owned hundreds of slaves.

The Washingtons found a way to work around the law. They moved their slaves between their Philadelphia mansion and Mount Vernon at least every six months.

If Judge and the rest of their slaves left the state after six months, they would not be considered residents. Then this law would not apply to them.

THE FUGITIVE SLAVE ACTS

Enslaved people sometimes tried to escape to earn their freedom. But running away did not guarantee a person's freedom. People who escaped slavery were called fugitive slaves. Fugitive slaves were at risk of being captured. Laws called the Fugitive Slave Acts allowed slaveholders to search for their slaves and bring them back. The first Fugitive Slave Act was passed in 1793. It said that local governments could capture fugitive slaves and return them to their owners. Governments could punish anyone who tried to help fugitive slaves escape.

MAKING FRIENDS

Judge was often out and about in Philadelphia. She joined the Washingtons on social outings, where she often met servants and enslaved people. These outings helped Judge learn

THE AFRICAN AMERICAN POPULATION

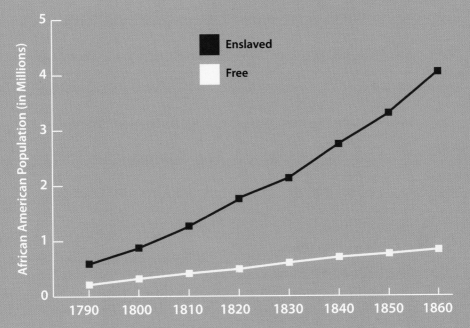

The above graph shows the number of enslaved and free African Americans in the United States from 1790 and 1860. How did these populations change throughout this time period? What do you think may have caused these changes?

more about the world outside of the Washingtons' home. Over time, Judge heard about the Pennsylvania law. She began to understand what it might be like to have freedom. Still she was cautious. If the Washingtons caught her talking about freedom, they might send her back to Mount Vernon permanently.

In the late 1700s, there was a growing free black community in Philadelphia. Philadelphia was largely a safe place for people of African descent to live since many of the city's residents were against slavery. Many jobs were available for black people. Some black people worked as domestic servants and day laborers. Others worked as teachers or doctors. Judge observed how these people lived. She admired their freedom.

The Free African Society (FAS) supported the free black community in Philadelphia. Two African American preachers founded this group in 1787. The FAS taught African Americans how to read. It cared for people in the black community who were sick or had lost a family member. Judge came to know some FAS members. These people helped Judge plan her escape.

ESCAPE TO PORTSMOUTH

Judge had thought about running away before. But compared with other enslaved people, Judge felt she lived a fairly comfortable life. Martha often treated

Today the slave quarters at Mount Vernon show how Judge and other people enslaved by the Washingtons may have lived.

Judge as if she were her own child. But all that changed when Judge heard she would be given to Martha's granddaughter, Eliza. Judge then realized that the Washingtons thought of her as their property.

Judge made her plans with the help of free African Americans in Philadelphia. Some historians think Richard Allen, one of the founders of the FAS, helped Judge escape. Judge may have met Allen when he did work on the Washingtons' chimney.

On May 21, 1796, Judge escaped the presidential mansion. She walked to the Delaware River and

HARRIET JACOBS

Enslaved people who made the journey to freedom often did not know what to expect. Harriet Jacobs was enslaved in North Carolina. She escaped her slaveholder in 1835. She hid for seven years in her grandmother's attic before she finally felt safe enough to leave. She traveled to Philadelphia in a boat with another escaped slave. In her autobiography *Incidents in the Life of a Slave Girl*, Jacobs described the moment they landed in the new city. She said, "Before us lay the city of strangers. We had escaped from slavery. . . . But we were alone in the world."

boarded a ship called the *Nancy*.

The journey on the *Nancy* took Judge from the Delaware River into the Atlantic Ocean. The boat was packed with goods and other passengers. It sailed along the East Coast. It made a brief stop in New York. From there, the boat traveled to Portsmouth, New Hampshire. The journey took five days. Once in Portsmouth, Judge would start her new life.

STRAIGHT TO THE
SOURCE

When enslaved people ran away, slaveholders placed newspaper advertisements. These ads were meant to help them find the slaves. The Washingtons placed an ad for Judge in the *Pennsylvania Gazette* in May 1796. It read:

Absconded from the household of the President of the United States, ONEY JUDGE, a light mulatto girl, much freckled, with very black eyes and bushy black hair. She is of middle stature, slender, and delicately formed, about 20 years of age. . . . Ten dollars will be paid to any person who will bring her home, if taken in the city, or on board any vessel in the harbour;—and a reasonable additional sum if apprehended at, and brought from a greater distance, and in proportion to the distance.

Source: Sarah Pierson. "Ona Judge." *Mount Vernon Ladies' Association.* Mount Vernon.org, n.d. Web. Accessed July 18, 2018.

What's the Big Idea?
Carefully read this advertisement. What is the advertisement asking people to look for? How would a person be rewarded if they found Judge?

CHAPTER FIVE

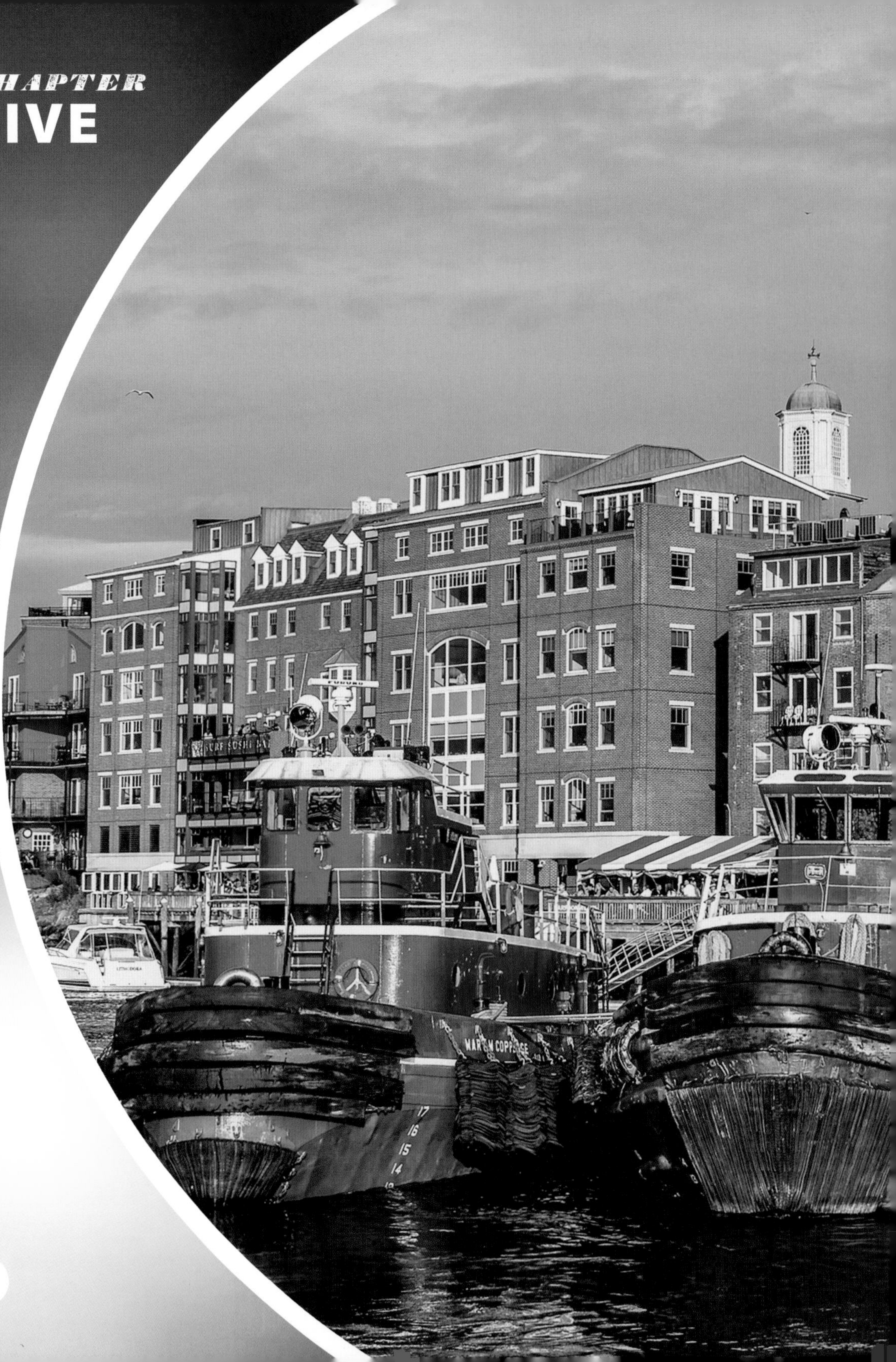

LATER LIFE AND LEGACY

Portsmouth was a small city. Approximately 5,000 people lived there. Judge did not know anything about Portsmouth. But it did not take long for her to find her place. Portsmouth had been one of the first places in New Hampshire to end the practice of slavery. The free black people there helped Judge find a home and work.

Judge took a job as a domestic servant. The work was difficult. Judge scrubbed floors, cooked meals, and carried heavy loads. In her free time, she taught herself to read and write.

Today Portsmouth, New Hampshire, remains an important harbor city.

In January 1797, Judge married a free man named Jack Staines. She took his last name and became Oney Judge Staines. Judge's daughter Eliza was born in 1798.

ATTEMPTS TO CAPTURE JUDGE

Martha Washington was angry when she discovered that Judge had run away. She believed that someone must have convinced Judge to leave. The Washingtons would soon learn where Judge was hiding.

A few months after her arrival in Portsmouth, Judge was walking in the city. A young woman named Elizabeth Langdon spotted Judge. Langdon knew

UNDERGROUND RAILROAD

One of the best-known methods of escape in the 1800s was the Underground Railroad. This was not an actual railroad. It was a network of people who helped enslaved people travel to freedom. Historians believe this network was created in the late 1700s. Before Judge's escape, another person the Washingtons had enslaved had used this network to escape.

the Washingtons. She told the Washingtons what she had seen.

George Washington tried to bring Judge back. Washington enlisted the help of a man named Joseph Whipple. Whipple met with Judge and asked her to return to the Washingtons. She told him that she might go back if the Washingtons promised to free her after their deaths. The Washingtons would not agree to this condition, so Judge remained in Portsmouth.

George's nephew, Burwell Bassett Jr., also tried to capture Judge. Bassett came to Portsmouth in 1799. His goal was to bring Judge and her daughter Eliza to the Washingtons. John Langdon, Elizabeth Langdon's father, helped Judge. He was a former slaveholder. But his position on slavery had changed. John warned Judge about Bassett's plan.

A NEW TOWN

Judge fled Portsmouth with Eliza. Jack did not come with them at first. He worked as a sailor and was out at

John Langdon was a US senator who lived in Portsmouth, New Hampshire.

sea when Judge and Eliza traveled to the nearby city of Greenland, New Hampshire. Jack later joined them. They settled permanently in Greenland. Judge gave birth to her son William in 1800. Two years later, Judge's daughter Nancy was born.

Life was hard for Judge and her family. Jack died in 1803. Judge worked as a servant for many years. But she could not earn enough money to support her children. She arranged for her daughters to become servants for a white family. Judge's son left home to become a sailor.

By the time Judge reached the age of 50, she was living alone. Domestic work was often the only way for African American women to earn a living at the time. But Judge was no longer able to do tough physical labor. She relied on the charity of others. Judge died in Greenland in February 1848.

JUDGE'S LEGACY

For many years, few people had heard of Judge. Judge did not tell many people her story because she wanted to avoid capture and protect the people who had helped her escape. She gave interviews later in her life but otherwise tried to stay out of the public eye.

Many people began to learn about Judge in 2008. The presidential mansion in Philadelphia was rebuilt in that year. Exhibits in the mansion tell the stories of people whom the Washingtons had enslaved. One of those stories is Judge's.

Today many people work to educate the public about Judge and her legacy. In 2017 historian

Erica Armstrong Dunbar wrote a book about Judge's life. Judge's story was also included in an exhibit at Mount Vernon. In Portsmouth, an organization called the Portsmouth Black Heritage Trail created a tour. On the tour, people can visit places Judge may have lived and worked.

Judge was not considered free in the eyes of the law. Still, she lived many years as a woman in control of her own life. She started a family. Though she lived a life of poverty, she worked hard and earned money. And she gained what she wanted most. She finally felt free.

STRAIGHT TO THE
SOURCE

In 1846 Judge spoke with abolitionist Benjamin
Chase. Chase wrote about their meeting in a letter to the
editor of *The Liberator*:

> *I have recently made a visit to one of Gen. Washington's,
> or rather Mrs. Washington's slaves. [She] is a woman, nearly
> white, very much freckled, and probably, (for she does not
> know her age,) more than eighty. . . .*
>
> *She says that she was a chambermaid for Mrs. Washington . . .
> that when Washington was elected President, she was taken to
> Philadelphia, and that, although well enough used as to work and
> living, she did not want to be a slave always, and she supposed
> if she went back to Virginia, she would never have a chance
> of escape.*
>
> Source: John Blassingame. *Slave Testimony: Two Centuries
> of Letters, Speeches, Interviews, and Autobiographies.* Baton
> Rouge, LA: LSU Press, 2009. Print. 248–249.

Consider Your Audience

Adapt this passage for a different audience, such as your
principal or friends. Write a blog post conveying this
same information for the new audience. How does
your post differ from the original text and why?

FAST FACTS

- George and Martha Washington held Ona "Oney" Judge as a slave in the late 1700s. Oney was enslaved at birth. She began working as Martha's personal maid when she was ten years old.

- George became president in 1789. The Washingtons moved to New York. They took Judge and six other enslaved people with them.

- In 1790 the Washingtons and their slaves moved to Philadelphia, Pennsylvania.

- In Philadelphia, Judge met free African Americans who inspired her to escape.

- Martha decided to give Judge to her granddaughter as a wedding gift.

- Judge escaped from the presidential mansion on May 21, 1796. She boarded a ship and sailed to Portsmouth, New Hampshire.

- The Washingtons used different methods to try to reenslave Judge. Judge fled to Greenland, New Hampshire, to avoid capture.

- Judge had three children. She worked as a domestic servant for many years. She died in Greenland on February 25, 1848.

"I am free now"

Oney Judge's strong desire for freed[om]
22-year-old enslaved seamstress to [escape President Washington's]
House on May 21, 1796. With the [help of free people of]
African descent, she found passag[e to New Hampshire]
where she married, raised a famil[y...]

"Whilst they were packing up to [go to Virginia, I was]
packing to go, I didn't know w[here to, for I knew that if]
I went back to Virginia, I sho[uld never get my liberty.]
I had friends among the col[oured people of Philadelphia,]
had my things carried th[ere beforehand, and left]
Washington's house wh[ile they were eating dinner."]

STOP AND
THINK

Tell the Tale

Chapter Four discusses Judge's journey by ship from Philadelphia to Portsmouth. Imagine that you had to make a similar escape in the late 1700s. Write 200 words about your experience. How do you think you would feel as you made your escape? Do you think Judge had similar feelings?

Surprise Me

Chapter Two discusses slavery in early America. After reading this book, what two or three facts about slavery did you find most surprising? Write a few sentences about each fact. Why did you find each fact surprising?

Why Do I Care?

Enslaved people were freed in the United States after the Civil War (1861–1865). But slavery left a lasting legacy in the country. How might the United States be different today if slavery had not existed? How might your life be different?

GLOSSARY

abolitionist
someone who is
against slavery

colony
land owned by a faraway
country or nation

day laborers
workers who are paid one
day at a time with no set
term of employment

domestic servants
people who work inside the
homes of other people

fugitive
a person who has
broken a law and is
in hiding

indentured servant
a person who works for free
for a set amount of time

poverty
the condition of being
very poor

ONLINE
RESOURCES

To learn more about Oney Judge, **visit our free** resource
websites below.

Visit **abdocorelibrary.com** for free Common Core resources for teachers
and students, including vetted activities, multimedia, and booklinks, for
deeper subject comprehension.

Visit **abdobooklinks.com** for free additional online weblinks for further
learning. These links are routinely monitored and updated to provide
the most current information available.

LEARN
MORE

Rissman, Rebecca. *Slavery in the United States*. Minneapolis, MN: Abdo
    Publishing Company, 2015.

Woelfle, Gretchen. *Answering the Cry for Freedom*. Honesdale, PA:
    Calkins Creek, 2016.

ABOUT THE
AUTHORS

Duchess Harris, JD, PhD

Professor Harris is the chair of
the American Studies department
at Macalester College and curator
of the Duchess Harris Collection of
ABDO books. She is the author and
coauthor of recently released ABDO
books including *Hidden Human
Computers: The Black Women
of NASA*, *Black Lives Matter*, and *Race
and Policing*.

Before working with ABDO, she authored several other books on the
topics of race, culture, and American history. She served as an associate
editor for *Litigation News*, the American Bar Association Section of
Litigation's quarterly flagship publication, and was the first editor in
chief of *Law Raza*, an interactive online journal covering race and the
law, published at William Mitchell College of Law. She has earned a PhD
in American Studies from the University of Minnesota and a JD from
William Mitchell College of Law.

Lindsay Wyskowski

Lindsay Wyskowski is a writer and lifelong reader from
Michigan. She has a master's degree in public relations. She
enjoys writing stories to help others learn about new and
interesting subjects.

INDEX